Genre Realistic

MW01104946

Essential Questi...
How can you use wh...
to help others?

Stepping Forward

by Katharine Philipson

illustrated by Cheryl Cook

Chapter 1
My Favorite Thing

I love maps. Sometimes my friends tease about it. I don't mind that because they are just kidding, and, anyway, my mom says that it's good to have a hobby. She loves the stars the way I love maps. She spends hours every clear night studying them through her telescope. I'm even named Rigel after a star.

Rigel is the brightest star in the Orion Constellation. It is also one of the brightest stars in the sky. Mom says she called me Rigel because I'm her bright star. The other bright star in the Orion constellation is Betelgeuse. I'm glad she didn't name me after that one!

My friends may not understand my fascination with maps, but I guess they have hobbies that I find boring. Seb—it's short for Sebastian—loves to go fishing. He can spend hours sitting in a boat. Liana is crazy about computer games. But there are things we all like to do. We play basketball for hours. We go on bike rides, and we've formed a band. I play drums.

Anyway, as I said, I love maps—ancient maps, modern maps, world maps, city maps. My favorites are the maps made by Lewis and Clark during their transcontinental expedition in the early 1800s. I often imagine what it must have felt like to be part of that expedition. They must have felt so proud of their achievement.

I'm really looking forward to school today. The class is going on an orienteering hike. I've never been orienteering before. Orienteers find their way around a course using a map and a compass. It's a great way to practice reading a map.

Liana and Seb are already at school when I get there. Liana is just about dancing with excitement. Seb looks uncertain. He says he's unadventurous, but I think he just gets nervous when he is trying something new. Once he starts something, he's the most adventurous of all of us—he was the first one to go on the zip line at camp last year.

Chapter 2
Kevin Leads the Way

We take a bus to the orienteering course. It's in an area of forest and farmland about 30 miles from school. The sky is overcast, so I'm hoping it doesn't rain. When we get there, our teacher divides the class into four groups of five. Liana, Seb, and I are in a group with Atsuko and Kevin. A teacher is assigned to go with each group.

The guide hands a map and a compass to each group. She tells us that the course usually takes about two hours. She explains that we should pass three checkpoints on the way. We need to use the hole punch at each checkpoint to punch our cards. The guide says that there are two essential things to remember. First, orienteering is as much about reading a map properly as it is about speed. She says it is important to take the time to look at the map and plan our route. Second, we must stay together.

The art teacher, Mr. Lewis, is working with our group. He doesn't know us well, so he asks who wants to be leader. Liana is standing next to me. She digs me in the ribs.

"Go on," she says. "Put up your hand!"

I'm too embarrassed to volunteer. I don't like to be the center of attention. Kevin, the class know-it-all, is waving his hand in the air.

"I will! I will!" he shouts. "I know all about orienteering."

Mr. Lewis gives Kevin the map and compass.

"Lead on!" he says after making sure that everyone is wearing a jacket, hat, and gloves.

Kevin is much too impatient to take the time to read the map and plan the route.

"We'll head to that hill," he declares. "Then we'll be able to see which way to go."

"But what about the map?" I ask.

"I told you, I've done this before. You don't need a map," he replies with confidence.

Then Kevin takes off. We have to run to keep up with him. Instead of staying together, we are spread out behind Kevin. Poor Mr. Lewis is running back and forth like a mother duck, trying to keep an eye on everyone.

We've been walking for a long time, and I'm sure that by now we should have reached the first checkpoint. Soon we realize that between us and the hill is a swamp.

"We'll just go through it," Kevin announces. "It doesn't look bad."

"Nonsense!" snaps Mr. Lewis, looking annoyed. "It looks very unsafe. We'll go around it."

This time Kevin does look at the map before he sets off. "There's a track around this side," he says.

We set off again. The path gets muddier and muddier. When we have been going for nearly an hour, I look at where the sun is and realize we are heading northwest instead of southeast.

"Excuse me, Mr. Lewis," I say. "I apologize for interrupting, but I think we're going in the wrong direction."

"Let me see the map, please, Kevin," says Mr. Lewis. "You're right, Rigel. Why don't you lead the way for a while?"

Chapter 3
Back on Track

Kevin hands over the map and the compass. I detect a slight look of relief on his face. I check our direction on the compass, and then look at the map. I see that we are definitely off track. We could retrace our steps back to the beginning of the course and start again. However, it's getting late. Everyone will start to worry if we are very late getting back.

There is another option, though. It is a more complicated route than the official course, but if we follow it, we will eventually join the path we should be on. We will miss two checkpoints, which means we will be disqualified, but that seems a small price to pay if we can get back safely before someone decides to send out a search party.

I give Kevin the compass and show him the direction in which we should be heading. I would be happier if Liana or Seb were carrying it, but Kevin looks a bit embarrassed, and he might feel better if he helps to get us back on course.

We skirt the other side of the swamp until we get to a gate. We go through the gate and take a rather overgrown trail through the woods. Mr. Lewis is a bit doubtful when he sees the state of the trail, but I show him where the trail is marked on the map and where it joins the path we should be on. Then Kevin shows him the compass, and he begins to look more comfortable.

I make sure everyone stays together, even though Kevin still likes to be out in front of everyone else and Atsuko and Liana keep falling behind. They are convinced that if they look hard enough, they will find some prehistoric remains among the trees. The trail gets more overgrown as we get farther into the woods. I am beginning to doubt my own map-reading skills.

Just as I am beginning to wonder if we have missed the path, it appears. The trail joins the path just before the last checkpoint. We punch our card to show we have passed by. Everyone sets off on the last stage with renewed energy.

Of course, we are the last group to get to the end of the course, but that's okay. After all, we've hiked a lot farther than anyone else!

Chapter 4
I Share My Hobby

The next day at school, everyone is talking about our adventure. I seem to be the hero of the moment. Some of the kids ask me about maps. Our teacher, Ms. Day, overhears us talking. She says she has heard that my map-reading talents saved the day on the orienteering hike. In class, Ms. Day asks how many people can read a map. Only a few of us put up our hands. One of them is Kevin—he seems to have regained his confidence.

Ms. Day decides that we will study maps. We will learn the history of maps and how important they are. She explains that being able to read a map and use a compass could save someone's life one day. Everyone in the class will learn how to read a map. Then our assignment will be to map our neighborhood.

Seb tells Ms. Day about my map collection. She asks if I could bring some of my maps to school and talk to the class about them.

I take my special maps to school the next day. I tell the class about Lewis and Clark and their daring overland expedition. I talk about Christopher Columbus and other explorers, and how they made maps of the places they discovered. I explain that maps aren't just for Earth. Astronomers map the sky, too. I tell them about Mom and her fascination with the stars.

When I finish my talk, lots of people ask questions. They are really interested. Ms. Day asks if Mom would give a talk to the class about finding the way using the sun and the stars. I say that I'm sure she'd be delighted.

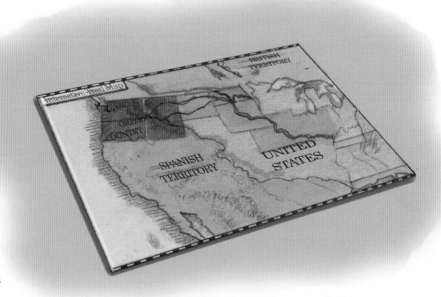

That day, my class learned all about the importance of maps and how fascinating they could be. I learned something, too. I learned that I'm more confident than I thought, and that sometimes it feels good to talk in front of an audience.

Respond to Reading

Summarize

Use details from the story to summarize the important events in *Stepping Forward*. The details from your Point of View Chart may help you summarize.

Details

↓

Point of View

Text Evidence

1. How do you know that *Stepping Forward* is realistic fiction? Use examples from the story to support your answer. GENRE

2. How do you know that the story is told through Rigel's eyes? Give two examples. POINT OF VIEW

3. Find the word *impatient* on page 8. How does the prefix *im-* help you figure out the meaning? PREFIXES

4. Imagine that you were Kevin in *Stepping Forward*. Write three sentences about the orienteering hike from Kevin's point of view. WRITE ABOUT READING

Compare Texts
Read another story about Rigel.

Rigel to the Rescue

"Guess what, Mom?" shouted Rigel. "Seb got us a gig for our band. They want us to open at a concert at the Larksville Community Center."

"Congratulations," said Mom. "When is this gig?"

"It's next Saturday, but there's a problem," Rigel said. "Seb's parents are away, Liana's father doesn't drive, and her mother will be at work."

"I'll take you," Mom said.

Rigel was unsure. At night, his mother could find her way anywhere by using the stars. However, during the day she had no sense of direction at all.

"It's okay," Mom said. "I grew up in Larksville. I know my way around there."

Illustration: Cheryl Cook

17

On the Saturday of the concert, they set off with plenty of time to spare.

"Are you sure you know the way, Ms. Edwards?" asked Seb. He'd been Rigel's friend since they were little, so he'd been lost with Rigel's mom quite often.

"Yes, I remember Larksville well," she replied.

They arrived in Larksville, and Ms. Edwards drove confidently toward the center of town. She pulled up outside a small building.

"Here you are," she said.

Rigel, Liana, and Seb looked at the run-down building. "I don't think so," said Rigel, beginning to feel worried.

"How long since you were last here?" asked Liana.

"It must be 25 years—we moved from here when I was about 12," Ms. Edwards said.

Rigel began to panic. They were due to perform in an hour, and they needed 20 minutes to set up.

"Perhaps they've built a new community center," Seb suggested.

Rigel had an idea. "They often mark public buildings on a map," he said. "Let's have a look."

Sure enough, "community center" was on the map in red print—but it was miles away.

"OK, Rigel," said his mom, sounding very businesslike. "I'll drive. You direct me."

They arrived at the community center with just enough time to set up but not enough time to get too nervous. When they finished their gig, everyone clapped. Rigel's mom clapped hardest of all.

As they put their gear into the car, Rigel asked, "Hey, Mom, can you find your way home?"

Rigel's mom grinned and said, "Well, if I can't, at least I've got the best map reader in town with me."

Make Connections

What was the problem in *Rigel to the Rescue*? How did Rigel use his talent to solve it? ESSENTIAL QUESTION

What do think was the main message in *Stepping Forward* and *Rigel to the Rescue*? TEXT TO TEXT

Focus on Genre

Realistic Fiction *Stepping Forward* and *Rigel to the Rescue* are realistic fiction. Stories in this genre are often set in the present. The characters are realistic. That means that they are like real people.

Read and Find Find two examples in the story that show that *Stepping Forward* is realistic fiction. How does the author show that the story takes place in the present? How does the author make the characters seem like real people?

Your Turn

Write an imaginary story about using a talent or skill to solve a problem. First, think of a realistic problem that your character might have. Then think of a skill or talent that could solve the problem. Although the story is imaginary, the talent or skill should be realistic, not far-fetched. Write the story in the first person, as if you are the main character.